GW01236835

SPMG

HEINEMANN MATHEMATICS 6

Heinemann Mathematics 6 is intended for use with children
• working mainly at Level 4 of the National Curriculum (England and Wales) and Common Curriculum (Northern Ireland)
• working towards Level D of Mathematics 5–14 (Scotland).

Heinemann

Heinemann Educational,
A Division of Heinemann Publishers (Oxford) Ltd,
Halley Court, Jordan Hill, Oxford OX2 8EJ

OXFORD   LONDON   EDINBURGH
MADRID   ATHENS   BOLOGNA   PARIS
MELBOURNE   SYDNEY   AUCKLAND   SINGAPORE   TOKYO
IBADAN   NAIROBI   HARARE   GABORONE
PORTSMOUTH NH (USA)

ISBN 0 435 02231 8

© Scottish Primary Mathematics Group 1995
First published 1995
99 98 97 96 95
10 9 8 7 6 5 4 3 2

Writing Team
John T Blair
Ian K Clark
Aileen P Duncan
Percy W Farren
Archie MacCallum
John Mackinlay
Myra A Pearson
Catherine D J Preston
Dorothy S Simpson
John W Thayers
David K Thomson

Designed and produced by Oxprint Ltd
Printed in the UK by Athenaeum Press Ltd, Gateshead, Tyne & Wear.

Introduction

■ This booklet contains 30 photocopiable reinforcement sheets designed to provide further practice in selected topics for children using Heinemann Mathematics 6.

■ Each sheet is referenced from a specific page of Heinemann Mathematics 6 Textbook or Workbook and is designed to supplement the mathematics of the section from which it is referenced. For example, page 24 of the Textbook carries the symbol $\boxed{\textbf{R}\,7}$

to indicate that reinforcement sheet 7 is available to provide further practice in the aspect dealt with in that section, ie division of HTU and ThHTU by 6, 7, 8, 9.

■ The top right-hand corner of each reinforcement sheet states the mathematical topic and the core page from which it is referenced. For example,

Division: HTU and ThHTU by 6, 7, 8, 9
Heinemann Mathematics 6 **Textbook, page 24**

■ A list of the sheets, with the mathematical topics they cover and references to Textbook and Workbook pages, is given on the next page.

References to the curriculum are not provided in this booklet. The appropriate references are those of the core pages to which the sheets are linked and can be found in the Teacher's Notes.

■ The Teacher's Notes list reinforcement sheets in the Overview section for each mathematical topic. The 'R' symbol described above also appears beside the notes for any core page which has an associated reinforcement sheet.

■ There are no teaching notes for reinforcement sheets. Their content is similar to that of their associated core pages, for which introductory activities appear in the Teacher's Notes.

■ Each sheet is intended to be used *selectively* with those children who show a need for some extra practice over and above that provided in the core materials.

There is no advantage in using the sheets routinely with children who have already mastered the work. They would be better engaged in using the Extension Textbook, the Problem Solving Activities in the Assessment and Resources Pack, or in tackling a new topic.

The sheets are not designed to assist those pupils whose understanding of the topic is so poor that they really require further teaching before engaging in more practice.

■ In most cases the reinforcement sheets continue the *context* of the core section to which they relate. This is intended to make it easier to integrate them with on-going work when supplementary examples are required for some children.

■ Some of the sheets have a fill-in format. A 'pencil' symbol appears beside the number of the sheet in these cases. **8** ✏

■ The only materials required are calculators, coloured pencils, scissors and glue.

■ Answers for the reinforcement sheets are provided at the end of this booklet.

Mathematical content

On the beach

These are the numbers of items collected on the beach.

round pebbles 45

flat pebbles 8

white shells 134

pink shells 7

1 Find **mentally:**
   (a) the total number of • pebbles • shells
   (b) the difference between the numbers of
       • round pebbles and flat pebbles • white shells and pink shells.

2 Add or subtract **mentally.**
   (a) 56 + 23   (b) 78 − 52   (c) 34 + 65   (d) 89 − 66   (e) 27 + 61
   (f) 96 − 84   (g) 75 + 14   (h) 36 − 16   (i) 62 + 36   (j) 92 − 81

3 Sean gathered 48 pieces of wood for the bonfire. Roy gathered 30.
   Calculate **mentally.**
   (a) How many pieces of wood were gathered altogether?
   (b) How many more pieces did Sean gather than Roy?

4 Add or subtract **mentally.**
   (a) 25 + 40   (b) 95 − 60   (c) 32 + 60   (d) 88 − 80   (e) 46 + 50
   (f) 37 − 20   (g) 64 + 20   (h) 74 − 50   (i) 17 + 70   (j) 63 − 30

Dorothy and Elaine counted the beach wildlife they saw.

gulls 45

crabs 54

parrots 28

baby turtles 27

5 Calculate **mentally.**
   (a) How many **birds** were counted altogether?
   (b) What was the total number of crabs and turtles?
   (c) How many more gulls than parrots were counted?
   (d) What was the difference between the numbers of turtles and crabs?

6 Add or subtract **mentally.**
   (a) 35 + 58   (b) 32 − 13   (c) 63 + 18   (d) 44 − 28   (e) 57 + 24
   (f) 84 − 55   (g) 48 + 29   (h) 62 − 42   (i) 36 + 37   (j) 45 − 16
   (k) 18 + 44   (l) 50 − 26   (m) 27 + 27   (n) 91 − 76   (o) 22 + 68

Large numbers

1 Write these numbers in figures.
  (a) eighty-two thousand, three hundred and forty-five
  (b) three hundred and fifty thousand
  (c) four hundred thousand and forty
  (d) one million, two hundred thousand
  (e) three million and ten

2 Write these numbers in words.
  (a) 73 000   **(b)** 393 500   **(c)** 202 202   **(d)** 6 000 600

3 Write the next three numbers in each sequence.
  (a) 9994, 9995, 9996, 9997. . .
  (b) 5000, 6000, 7000, 8000. . .
  (c) 99 600, 99 700, 99 800. . .
  (d) 100 060, 100 070, 100 080. . .
  (e) 999 996, 999 997, 999 998. . .

4 **Increase** 239 146 by
  (a) ten
  (b) ten thousand
  (c) two hundred thousand.

5 **Decrease** 763 994 by
  (a) two thousand
  (b) nine hundred
  (c) fifty thousand.

6 Write the number which is
  (a) 1 more than 24 999
  (b) 1 less than 300 000
  (c) 10 more than 110 000
  (d) 10 less than 77 700
  (e) 100 more than 90 900
  (f) 100 less than 1 000 500
  (g) 1000 more than 139 473
  (h) 1000 less than 50 001.

7 Write the value of the underlined digit in each number.
  (a) 2̲0 020   **(b)** 432̲ 100   **(c)** 2̲ 000 002
  (d) 5̲72 660   **(e)** 3 4̲00 044   **(f)** 395 6̲01
  (g) 4̲09 328   **(h)** 1̲0 003   **(i)** 5 55̲5 555

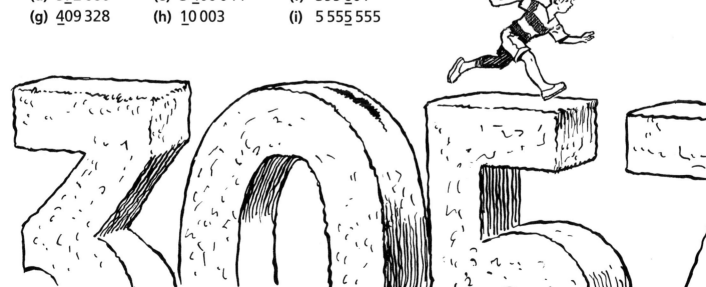

On the reef

These are the numbers of fish on the reef.

Jets 4892   **Goldies 4692**   **Gliders 6740**   **Zens 5309**

1 Find the total number of
   (a) striped fish   **(b)** spotted fish   **(c)** fish with pointed tails

2 Copy and complete.

(a)	(b)	(c)	(d)	(e)
1483	3745	1685	7895	7279
+ 4517	+ 6916	+ 5385	+ 3308	+ 8347

3 Add.
   (a) 938 + 7086   **(b)** 5283 + 620 + 1947   **(c)** 819 + 1038 + 76

4 On the reef, how many more Gliders are there than
   (a) Jets   **(b)** Goldies   **(c)** Zens?

5 Copy and complete.

(a)	(b)	(c)	(d)	(e)
4825	6313	4015	9415	2070
− 2062	− 3188	− 2071	− 7663	− 1388

(f)	(g)	(h)	(i)	(j)
3400	4009	2000	8000	5000
− 1154	− 1847	− 590	− 1423	− 2306

6 **(a)** Find the total number of • crabs • jellyfish.
   (b) How many more jellyfish than crabs are there?
   (c) How many more jellyfish are needed to make their total number 12 000?

Popeye crabs
3189

Common jellyfish
5093

Green jellyfish
5837

Orange crabs
4760

Corry crabs
308

Diving for treasure

These scales are on the control panel of the mini-sub.

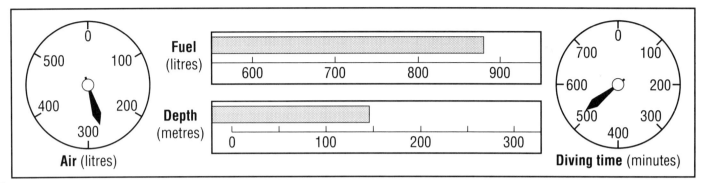

Air (litres)   **Fuel** (litres)   **Depth** (metres)   **Diving time** (minutes)

1 Read each scale **to the nearest hundred**. Copy and complete.

Air: about _____ litres   Fuel: about _____ litres

Depth: about _____ metres   Diving time: about _____ minutes

2 Round **to the nearest hundred**.

(a) 470   (b) 389   (c) 140   (d) 963   (e) 907   (f) 252

3 Round **to the nearest hundred** to estimate

(a) 186 + 430   (b) 120 + 595   (c) 325 + 217   (d) 415 + 276   (e) 392 + 189

(f) 643 − 119   (g) 586 − 294   (h) 920 − 436   (i) 712 − 289   (j) 865 − 359

silver coins **189**   rubies **122**   diamonds **33**   gold coins **72**

4 Round **to the nearest ten** the number of

(a) silver coins   (b) rubies   (c) diamonds   (d) gold coins.

5 Round **to the nearest ten** to estimate

(a) 139 + 54   (b) 41 + 226   (c) 164 + 77   (d) 79 + 248   (e) 291 + 32

(f) 292 − 29   (g) 366 − 38   (h) 169 − 83   (i) 257 − 41   (j) 225 − 57

6 By rounding **to the nearest ten**, estimate

(a) how many more rubies than diamonds there are

(b) the total number of coins.

Keeping warm

1 Mog uses money from the Earthquake Fund to buy clothes for the victims.

 scarves £3197

 hats £4299

 jackets £1064

 sweaters £1245

What is the cost of

(a) 3 vans of scarves   **(b)** 2 vans of hats   **(c)** 9 vans of jackets   **(d)** 6 vans of sweaters?

2 Mog makes some clothes.
She uses 4 boxes of zips,
        5 boxes of buttons,
        8 crates of cloth,
        7 boxes of thread.
How many of each item does she use?

 zips 2165

cloth 1209 rolls

buttons 1534

thread 1954 reels

3 **(a)** 2375 × 8   **(b)** 1879 × 5   **(c)** 2153 × 9   **(d)** 4837 × 4

4 To make one coat, Mog uses 6 metres of cloth and 8 buttons.
How many
(a) metres of cloth   **(b)** buttons
are used to make 1497 coats?

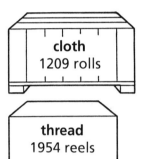

5 Mog's turbo-sew machine can make 2468 jackets
every hour.
How many jackets can it make in
(a) 7 hours   **(b)** 5 hours   **(c)** 8 hours?

6 Mog's machine puts 5 buttons on each coat instead of 8.
How many buttons altogether are missing from 2684 coats?

7 On each trip, Superhero delivers these clothes.

1628 coats
898 hats
3107 anoraks

How many of each item does
he deliver on
(a) 6 trips
(b) 9 trips
(c) 7 trips?

Emergency

1 Superhero shares these medical items equally into boxes.
How many items are in each box and how many are left over?

  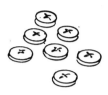

(a) 458 bottles into 3 boxes
(b) 590 bandages into 4 boxes
(c) 857 pills into 2 boxes
(d) 989 tablets into 5 boxes

2 (a) $1357 \div 2$ (b) $2635 \div 3$ (c) $3369 \div 4$ (d) $4051 \div 5$

(e) $4\overline{)3598}$ (f) $3\overline{)4479}$ (g) $5\overline{)2079}$ (h) $2\overline{)7535}$

3 Share 4561 splints equally into boxes.
How many are in each box and how many are left over when there are
(a) 3 boxes (b) 5 boxes (c) 4 boxes?

4 (a) $\frac{1}{2}$ of 7298 (b) $\frac{1}{3}$ of 8067 (c) $\frac{1}{5}$ of 8680 (d) $\frac{1}{4}$ of 7336

(e) $4\overline{)6009}$ (f) $5\overline{)3035}$ (g) $3\overline{)5234}$ (h) $2\overline{)9876}$

5 Superhero shares these items equally among trucks.

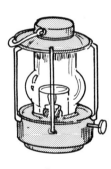  

6954 lamps   **3007 blankets**   **4269 tents**

How many of each item are in each truck and how many are left over when there are
(a) 2 trucks (b) 3 trucks (c) 4 trucks (d) 5 trucks?

6 There are 1476 cooking stoves.
One quarter of them are damaged.
How many stoves are damaged?

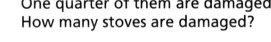

7 There are 9045 food parcels in Superhero's store.
He sends $\frac{1}{3}$ of them by plane.
How many parcels is this?

Robbers' loot

1 Superhero finds

	Total value
6 silver tankards	£990
7 gold chains	£973
8 bracelets	£856
9 rings	£711

What is the value of
(a) one tankard   (b) one gold chain   (c) one bracelet   (d) one ring?

2 (a) $6\overline{)1789}$ (b) $7\overline{)1098}$ (c) $8\overline{)2545}$ (d) $9\overline{)4539}$

(e) $8372 \div 8$ (f) $9600 \div 9$ (g) $9830 \div 8$ (h) $7589 \div 7$

3 Superhero finds 8737 beads.
How many beads are in each box
and how many are left over
when he shares them equally among
(a) 7 boxes   (b) 9 boxes?

4 (a) $\frac{1}{6}$ of 6882   (b) $\frac{1}{8}$ of 6048   (c) $\frac{1}{9}$ of 7587   (d) $\frac{1}{7}$ of 7189

(e) $4575 \div 7$ (f) $7390 \div 9$ (g) $3949 \div 8$ (h) $6820 \div 7$

5

Mog finds 2075 crystal glasses and
puts them into sets.
How many sets are there and
how many glasses are left over
when she puts them into
(a) sets of 6   (b) sets of 8?

6 The 6 robbers planned to share
their loot equally.
How many of each of these items
(a) should each robber have received
(b) would have been left over?

Robbers' loot	
4720 pens	765 clocks
2575 rings	830 watches

7 (a) Is 9 a factor of 4788? Explain.
(b) Is 8 a factor of 4788? Explain.

To the nearest unit

Complete • each calculation • each sentence • each number line.

---

254 ÷ 6 = _____

which is between _____ and _____ , or _____ to the nearest unit.

---

355 ÷ 7 = _____

which is between _____ and _____ , or _____ to the nearest unit.

---

307 ÷ 7 = _____

which is between _____ and _____ , or _____ to the nearest unit.

---

293 ÷ 8 = _____

which is between _____ and _____ , or _____ to the nearest unit.

---

587 ÷ 9 = _____

which is between _____ and _____ , or _____ to the nearest unit.

---

186 ÷ 7 = _____

which is between _____ and _____ , or _____ to the nearest unit.

---

697 ÷ 8 = _____

which is between _____ and _____ , or _____ to the nearest unit.

Catching the flight

Give each answer as a whole number.

1 How many journeys are needed to take 204 holidaymakers
to the airport in a coach which can seat
   (a) 12 people   **(b)** 16 people   **(c)** 18 people   **(d)** 23 people?

2 Give each answer **to the nearest unit**.
   (a) 346 ÷ 8   **(b)** 500 ÷ 9   **(c)** 3364 ÷ 13   **(d)** 4421 ÷ 17

3 In the airport lounge, holidaymakers sit in rows of 7.
How many **full** rows are there when there are
   (a) 224 people   **(b)** 204 people   **(c)** 188 people   **(d)** 249 people?

4 Luggage is taken to the airport in vans which can carry 72 cases.
How many journeys must be made to carry
   (a) 432 cases   **(b)** 585 cases   **(c)** 4080 cases   **(d)** 2051 cases?

5 **(a)** Each case is weighed at a check-in desk.
   Find, to the nearest kilogram, the average
   weight of a case on each of these flights:

| | Luggage | |
Flight	Total weight	Number of cases
Glasgow	2496 kg	156
Singapore	2060 kg	125
Toronto	3922 kg	201

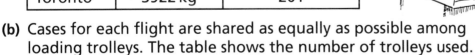

   (b) Cases for each flight are shared as equally as possible among
   loading trolleys. The table shows the number of trolleys used.

   For each flight, find to the nearest
   whole number, how many cases
   are on each trolley.

Flight	Cases	Trolleys
Glasgow	156	4
Singapore	125	3
Toronto	201	7

Equal fractions

1 Write equal fractions for each pair of designs.

(a)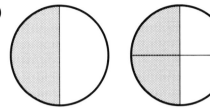

(b)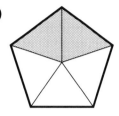

(c)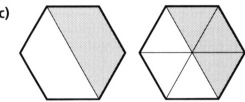

(d)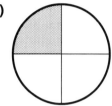

(e)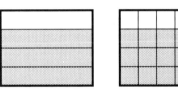

(f)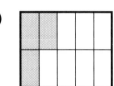

(g)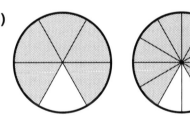

(h)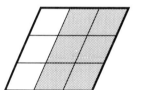

2 Find the missing numbers.

(a) $\frac{1}{2} = \frac{3}{6}$ $\times\square$ $\times\square$

(b) $\frac{3}{4} = \frac{15}{20}$ $\times\square$ $\times\square$

(c) $\frac{2}{3} = \frac{8}{12}$ $\times\square$ $\times\square$

3 Copy and complete.

(a) $\frac{1}{2} = \frac{}{8}$

(b) $\frac{2}{3} = \frac{}{6}$

(c) $\frac{1}{2} = \frac{}{12}$

(d) $\frac{1}{10} = \frac{}{100}$

(e) $\frac{1}{4} = \frac{}{12}$

(f) $\frac{3}{5} = \frac{}{10}$

(g) $\frac{4}{5} = \frac{}{20}$

(h) $\frac{1}{4} = \frac{}{20}$

(i) $\frac{7}{10} = \frac{}{20}$

(j) $\frac{4}{5} = \frac{}{10}$

(k) $\frac{3}{4} = \frac{}{12}$

(l) $\frac{9}{10} = \frac{}{100}$

4 Change (a) $\frac{3}{4}$ to eighths (b) $\frac{2}{3}$ to twelfths (c) $\frac{3}{10}$ to hundredths.

Equal fractions

1 Write equal fractions for each pair of designs.

(a)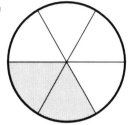

(b)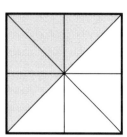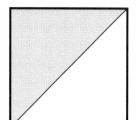

(c)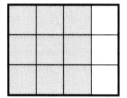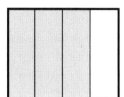

(d)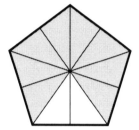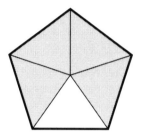

2 Copy and complete.

(a) $\dfrac{5}{10} = \dfrac{}{2}$ (b) $\dfrac{3}{9} = \dfrac{}{3}$ (c) $\dfrac{3}{12} = \dfrac{}{4}$ (d) $\dfrac{10}{20} = \dfrac{}{2}$

(e) $\dfrac{6}{9} = \dfrac{}{3}$ (f) $\dfrac{8}{12} = \dfrac{}{3}$ (g) $\dfrac{30}{100} = \dfrac{}{10}$ (h) $\dfrac{18}{20} = \dfrac{}{10}$

3 Change (a) $\dfrac{6}{12}$ to halves (b) $\dfrac{6}{8}$ to quarters (c) $\dfrac{4}{12}$ to thirds

(d) $\dfrac{4}{10}$ to fifths (e) $\dfrac{9}{12}$ to quarters (f) $\dfrac{8}{20}$ to fifths.

4 Simplify.

(a) $\dfrac{4}{6}$ (b) $\dfrac{2}{8}$ (c) $\dfrac{6}{10}$ (d) $\dfrac{4}{20}$ (e) $\dfrac{5}{20}$

(f) $\dfrac{10}{12}$ (g) $\dfrac{16}{20}$ (h) $\dfrac{50}{100}$ (i) $\dfrac{12}{20}$ (j) $\dfrac{70}{100}$

5 What fraction of the jugs are **(a)** full **(b)** empty?

6 There are 100 soldiers in the castle. Find the fraction of the soldiers who are on guard duty each day.

Number on guard duty		
Sunday	Monday	Tuesday
10	20	25

Name:

Division: second decimal place, notation

Heinemann Mathematics 6
Workbook page 10

Allt Bridge signs

1 Each sign has 100 light cells.
How much of each sign is lit? Write your answer
• as a fraction • in decimal form.

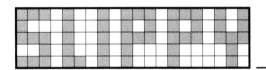   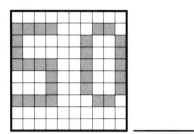

_____ _____   _____ _____

2 Write each fraction in decimal form.

13 hundredths _____   40 hundredths _____ $\frac{1}{100}$ _____ $\frac{10}{100}$ _____

3 Write each of these decimals in **two** other ways.

0·86 _____   0·90 _____   0·09 _____

4 Each sign has 100 light cells.
Colour to show the given fraction.

0·50   0·99

0·62   0·26   0·06

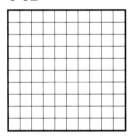   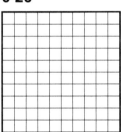   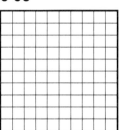   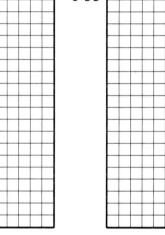

5 Colour to show the given amount.

1·42   2·20

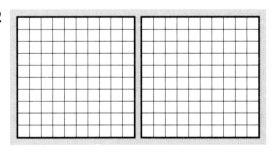   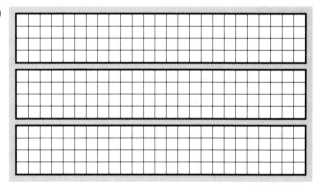

6 Write in decimal form:

3 units and 22 hundredths _____   4 units and 70 hundredths _____

3 units and 3 hundredths _____   5 units and 49 hundredths _____

Plants and posts

1 | 0·32 = 3 tenths and 2 hundredths |

Write each of these in the same way.
(a) 0·48   **(b)** 0·26   **(c)** 0·77   **(d)** 0·60   **(e)** 0·07

2 Write each of these in decimal form.
(a) 3 tenths and 6 hundredths
(b) 5 tenths and 8 hundredths
(c) 2 tenths and 0 hundredths
(d) 0 tenths and 9 hundredths
(e) 1 tenth and 1 hundredth

3 | 0·41 = 0·4 + 0·01 |

Write each of these in the same way.
(a) 0·67   **(b)** 0·37   **(c)** 0·80   **(d)** 0·04   **(e)** 0·66

4 Write the height of each plant in **(a)** m **(b)** cm.

5 Write the value of each shaded digit.
(a) 2·8 **3**   **(b)** **3** 2·42   **(c)** 12·**3** 2   **(d)** **3** ·61

6 **(a)** Write, in decimal form, the numbers shown in each row of the table.
(b) Write the numbers in order, from largest to smallest.
(c) Which of the numbers are between 3·6 and 0·6?

Units	tenths	hundredths
3	0	6
0	6	3
0	3	6
3	6	0
6	0	3

7 Write these numbers in order, from smallest to largest.
(a) 5·55, 0·5, 5·05, 0·55, 5·5
(b) 1·8, 0·60, 1·68, 0·81, 1·08

8 Which of these fence posts is **(a)** the longest **(b)** the shortest?

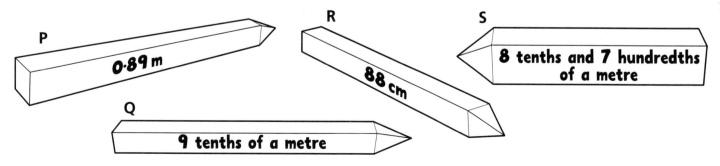

Euro-ferry

1 The Euro-ferry sign has 100 light cells. The chart shows the fraction of the sign lit by each of these symbols.

0·23	0·18	0·49	0·25	0·31

What fraction of the sign is lit when these symbols appear?

(a)    **(b)**    **(c)**    **(d)**

2
(a) 0·75 + 0·19
(b) 0·36 + 2·74
(c) 1·58 + 9·39
(d) 35·64 + 19·07
(e) 0·99 + 32·45
(f) 27·90 + 36·84

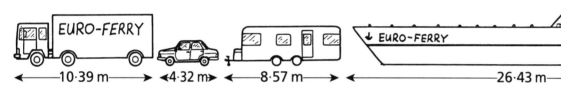

-10·39 m- -4·32 m- -8·57 m- -26·43 m-

3 How much longer is the boat than the **(a)** car   **(b)** caravan   **(c)** truck?

4
(a) 9·35 − 6·47
(b) 8·34 − 4·85
(c) 5·10 − 0·73
(d) 15·37 − 6·49
(e) 20·51 − 8·62
(f) 41·02 − 13·75

(g) 32·42 − 19·05   **(h)** 50·53 − 8·67   **(i)** 29·01 − 28·34   **(j)** 75·60 − 38·51

5 Find the difference in cost between
(a) an A-class cabin and a B-class cabin
(b) a B-class cabin and a C-class cabin
(c) a C-class cabin and a bunk
(d) an A-class cabin and a seat.

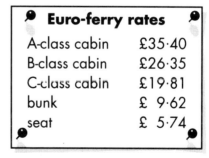

Euro-ferry rates

A-class cabin	£35·40
B-class cabin	£26·35
C-class cabin	£19·81
bunk	£ 9·62
seat	£ 5·74

6 Find the change from £50 after paying for
(a) an A-class cabin   **(b)** a bunk   **(c)** a C-class cabin.

7 The ferry charge for a truck is £50·85. What is the total cost for a truck and a C-class cabin for the driver?

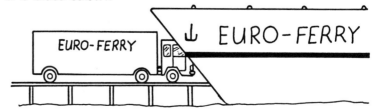

The Castle shop

Percentages: concept

Heinemann Mathematics 6
Workbook page 12

Patchwork quilts, each with 100 patches, are sold in the Castle shop.

1 For each quilt, find the percentage which is • grey • white

(a)

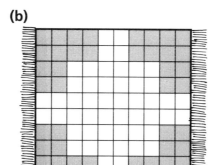

(b)

(c)

grey _____ %

white _____ %

_____

_____

_____

_____

2 Complete.

$20\% = \dfrac{\quad}{100}$ $75\% = \dfrac{\quad}{100}$

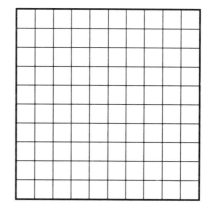

3 **(a)** Colour this quilt • 12% blue
                               • 20% red
                               • 50% green.

   (b) What percentage is **not** coloured? _____

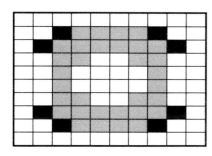

4 **(a)** What percentage of this quilt is

      • grey _____   • black? _____

   (b) Use red **and** green to colour the rest of
            the quilt.

   (c) Complete. _____ % is coloured red

                      _____ % is coloured green.

In the Castle shop

1 For each quilt, write
- the **fraction** grey
- the **percentage** grey.

(a)

(b)

(c)

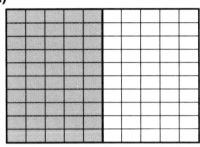

2 Copy and complete: **(a)** $50\% = \dfrac{1}{}$ **(b)** $25\% = \dfrac{}{}$ **(c)** $10\% = \dfrac{}{}$

3 Find

(a) 50% of 14	**(b)** 50% of 22	**(c)** 50% of 40	**(d)** 25% of 12
(e) 25% of 28	**(f)** 25% of 48	**(g)** 10% of 50	**(h)** 10% of 90
(i) 10% of 30	**(j)** 50% of 34	**(k)** 25% of 56	**(l)** 10% of 100

4 In each box, 50% of the pencils are green and 25% of the pencils are blue.
How many pencils in each box are
(a) green   **(b)** blue?

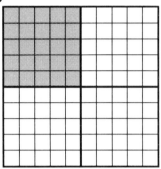

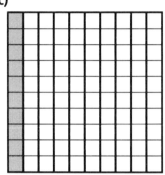

5 There are 300 postcards in the shop.
50% are large and 10% are small.
How many are **(a)** large   **(b)** small?

6 The shop has 80 quilts. 10% of the quilts are large, 50% are medium and the rest are small.

(a) **How many** quilts are   • medium   • large?

(b) **What percentage** of the quilts are small?

Patterns

Pattern: word formulae
Heinemann Mathematics 6 Workbook page 16

1 (a) Draw the next two **matchstick** patterns.

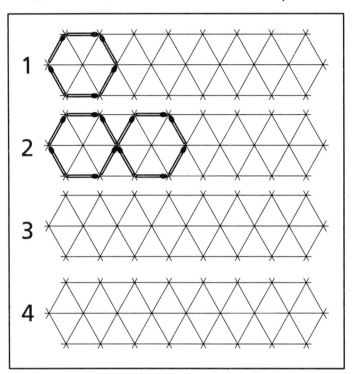

1

2

3

4

(b) Complete:

Number of hexagons	Number of matches
1 ⟶	6
2 ⟶	
3 ⟶	
4 ⟶	
5 ⟶	

(c) How many matches would be needed for
- 10 hexagons _____
- 100 hexagons? _____

(d) The number of matches is _____ times the number of hexagons.

2 (a) Colour the next two **cross** patterns.

1

2

3

4

(b) Complete:

Number of crosses	Number of coloured squares
1 ⟶	5
2 ⟶	
3	
4	
5	

(c) How many coloured squares would there be in
- 9 crosses _____
- 20 crosses? _____

(d) The number of coloured squares is _____ the number of crosses.

Departure lounges

1 Each departure lounge has 23 tables.
Copy and complete to find the number
of tables in 16 lounges.

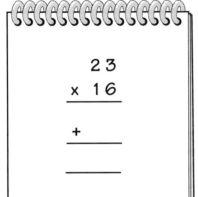

```
    2 3
x   1 6
_____

+
_____

_____
```

2 Find the number of tables in
   (a) 12 lounges   (b) 14 lounges   (c) 17 lounges.

3 (a)   32   (b)   47   (c)   61   (d)   58
         × 19   × 13   × 15   × 16

   (e)   74   (f)   69   (g)   29   (h)   33
         × 11   × 12   × 18   × 17

4 Each lounge has 49 chairs. How many chairs are
   in (a) 15 lounges (b) 18 lounges?

5 Trish arranges 35 white flowers,
   21 pink flowers and 46 peach
   flowers for each lounge.
   How many of each colour of flower
   does she arrange for
   (a) 11 lounges   (b) 13 lounges?

Playing the game

1 Copy and complete to find the score.

```
    4 5
  × 2 7

  +
  ─────

  ─────
```

2 (a) 23
× 45

(b) 37
× 53

(c) 86
× 26

(d) 56
× 71

(e) 62
× 39

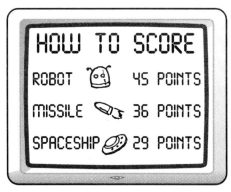

HOW TO SCORE

ROBOT   45 POINTS

MISSILE   36 POINTS

SPACESHIP 29 POINTS

3 Find the scores for hitting
   (a) 22 robots
   (b) 57 missiles
   (c) 76 spaceships
   (d) 41 missiles
   (e) 28 robots.

4 Find each amount.   **(a)** 26 × £43   **(b)** 95 × £37   **(c)** £84 × 66   **(d)** £48 × 51

5 Find the cost of
   (a) 24 mystery games
   (b) 38 sports games
   (c) 29 space adventures

£49

Mystery game

Space adventure £53

£44

Sports game

6 Multiply   **(a)** 31 × 36   **(b)** 25 × 43   **(c)** 19 × 28
             (d) 18 × 54   **(e)** 37 × 67   **(f)** 93 × 16

Going on board

1 Share 60 *Airways* magazines equally among 18 planes.
Copy and complete.

$$18\overline{)60}$$
$$-\,18\ \big|\ 1$$

There are _____ magazines for each plane

and _____ left over.

2 **(a)** $15\overline{)36}$ **(b)** $19\overline{)64}$ **(c)** $24\overline{)57}$

3 Share 163 copies of the *Lynchester Times* equally among 14 planes.
Copy and complete.

$$14\overline{)163}$$
$$-\,140\ \big|\ 10$$

There are _____ copies for each plane

and _____ left over.

4 **(a)** $16\overline{)189}$ **(b)** $19\overline{)203}$ **(c)** $21\overline{)250}$

  (d) $286 \div 23$ **(e)** $300 \div 27$ **(f)** $308 \div 28$

5 Share 400 children's packs equally among 18 planes.
How many are put on each plane and how many are left over?

6 **(a)** $17\overline{)369}$ **(b)** $22\overline{)470}$ **(c)** $24\overline{)500}$

  (d) $312 \div 26$ **(e)** $796 \div 25$ **(f)** $617 \div 29$

Spick and span

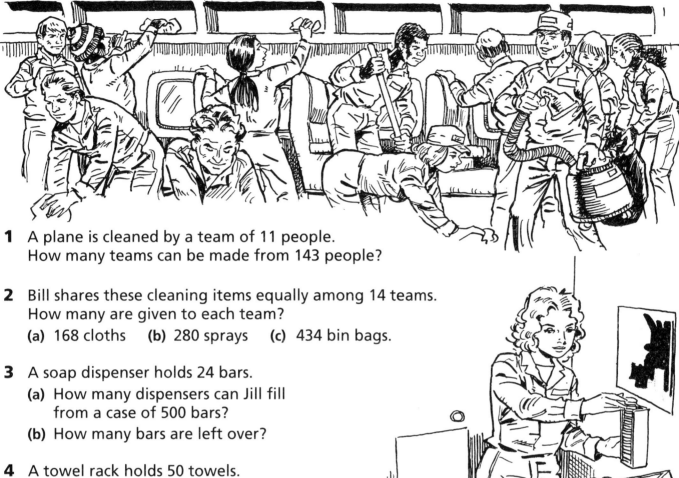

1 A plane is cleaned by a team of 11 people.
How many teams can be made from 143 people?

2 Bill shares these cleaning items equally among 14 teams.
How many are given to each team?
   (a) 168 cloths   **(b)** 280 sprays   **(c)** 434 bin bags.

3 A soap dispenser holds 24 bars.
   (a) How many dispensers can Jill fill
      from a case of 500 bars?
   (b) How many bars are left over?

4 A towel rack holds 50 towels.
How many racks can Jill fill
from a case of 600 towels?

5 Dave's team take 15 minutes to clean each plane.
They spent 315 minutes cleaning planes on Tuesday.
How many planes did they clean that day?

6 A team of 11 cleaners win a prize of £242.
The prize money is shared equally.
How much does each receive?

Lengths

1 Write the length of each roll of fencing in **centimetres**.

(a)  4 m 65 cm

(b) 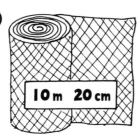 10 m 20 cm

(c) 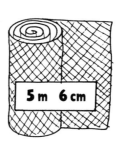 5 m 6 cm

(d) 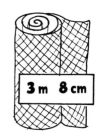 3 m 8 cm

2 Write in centimetres.
   (a) 3 m 45 cm   **(b)** 3 m 90 cm   **(c)** 7 m 5 cm   **(d)** $4\frac{1}{2}$ m

3 Write in metres and centimetres.
   (a) 265 cm   **(b)** 381 cm   **(c)** 340 cm   **(d)** 550 cm
   (e) 807 cm   **(f)** 605 cm   **(g)** 230 cm   **(h)** 306 cm

4 Find the perimeters of each animal enclosure.

(a) 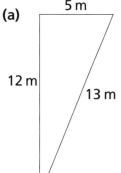 5 m, 12 m, 13 m

(b) 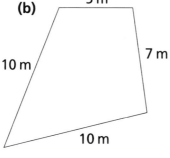 5 m, 10 m, 7 m, 10 m

(c) 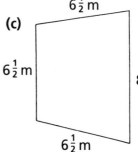 $6\frac{1}{2}$ m, $6\frac{1}{2}$ m, 8 m, $6\frac{1}{2}$ m

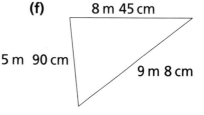

(d) 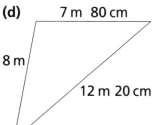 7 m 80 cm, 8 m, 12 m 20 cm

(e) 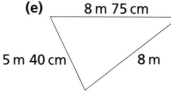 8 m 75 cm, 5 m 40 cm, 8 m

(f) 8 m 45 cm, 5 m 90 cm, 9 m 8 cm

5 Find the perimeter of each square enclosure.

(a) 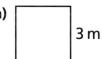 3 m

(b) 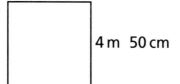 4 m 50 cm

(c)  5 m 75 cm

6 Find the perimeter of a square with a side length of
   (a) 7 m   **(b)** 62 cm   **(c)** 3 m 10 cm
   (d) 4 m 25 cm   **(e)** 6 m 9 cm   **(f)** $2\frac{1}{2}$ m

Name:

Just weight

Weight: scales
Heinemann Mathematics 6 Workbook page 24

1 Read the scales to find the weight of each of these.

(B) berries _____   (S) swede _____   (R) raisins _____

(A) apple _____   (N) nuts _____   (G) grapes _____

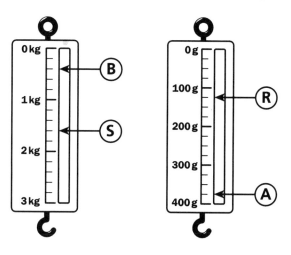
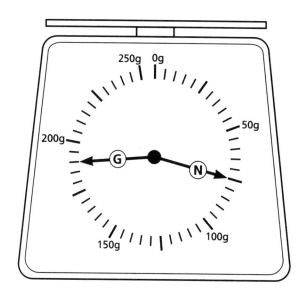

2 On the scales, draw pointers to show the weight of each egg.

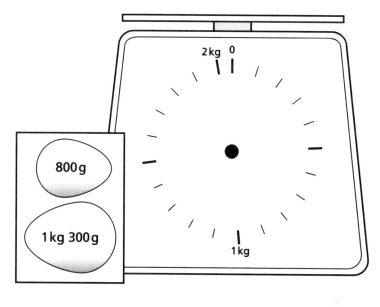
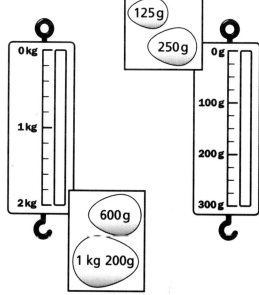

3 Write the weight of each animal, to the nearest mark.

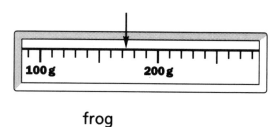

frog _____

lizard _____

More designs

Divide each design into squares and rectangles and find its area.

Area = _____ squares

Area = _____

Area = _____

Area = _____

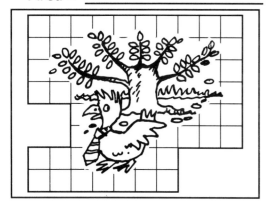

Area = _____

Area = _____

Area = _____

Area = _____

Medicines

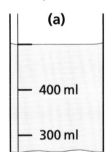

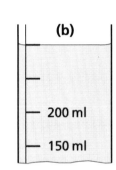

5 ml

50 ml

1 **(a)** A koala is given 15 ml of medicine each day. How many spoonfuls is this? _____

(b) A kangaroo is given 250 ml of medicine each day. How many tubfuls is this? _____

(c) After how many days will the kangaroo have had 1 litre of medicine? _____

2 Complete each scale.

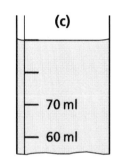

(a)
— 400 ml
— 300 ml

(b)
— 200 ml
— 150 ml

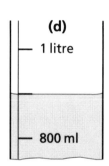

(c)
— 70 ml
— 60 ml

(d)
— 1 litre
— 800 ml

Find the volume, in millilitres, of each medicine.

(a) _____   **(b)** _____   **(c)** _____   **(d)** _____

3 Whose medicine is in each jar?

LION   260 ml
APE   275 ml
CROCODILE 310 ml

— 400 ml
— 300 ml
— 200 ml

— 300 ml
— 250 ml
— 200 ml
— 150 ml
— 100 ml

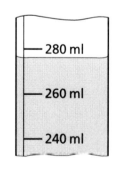

— 280 ml
— 260 ml
— 240 ml

(a) _____   **(b)** _____   **(c)** _____

4 Colour the jars to show each volume.

(a) 250 ml

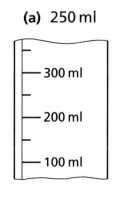

— 300 ml
— 200 ml
— 100 ml

(b) 90 ml

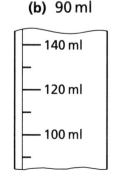

— 140 ml
— 120 ml
— 100 ml

(c) 680 ml

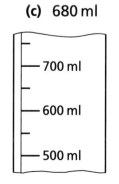

— 700 ml
— 600 ml
— 500 ml

Radio station

Class 6 used these timetables to plan a visit to the local radio station.

school to town centre	
depart	**arrive**
(a) 9.10 am —	9.50 am
(b) 9.35 am —	10.20 am
(c) 9.55 am —	10.45 am

town centre to radio station	
depart	**arrive**
(a) 10.00 am —	11.35 am
(b) 10.15 am —	12 noon
(c) 10.25 am —	12.15 pm
(d) 10.50 am —	12.40 pm

1 How many minutes does each bus take
to go from the school to the town centre?

2 How many minutes does each bus take
from the town centre to the radio station?

3 Find the earliest time Class 6 can arrive at the radio station if they take
(a) the 9.10 am bus   (b) the 9.35 am bus   (c) the 9.55 am bus.

4 Look at the Outside Broadcast schedule.
How long does each journey take?

Outside Broadcast Schedule		
Event	**Leave studio**	**Arrive at event**
(a) Sports day	9.10 am	10.50 am
(b) Baby show	9.20 am	11.10 am
(c) Lifeboats	7.15 am	11.05 am
(d) Royal visit	8.40 am	12.10 pm
(e) Speedway	8.55 am	2.45 pm

5 Jack, the director, leaves the radio station at 7.10 am and returns at 5.00 pm.
How long is he away from the station?

6 Robyn, the producer, leaves the radio station at 6.15 am and returns at 4.35 pm.
How long is she away from the station?

Channel

1 What is the **finishing time** for each of these recording sessions?

Studio	Starting time	Session lasts
A	9.30 am	25 minutes
B	10.15 am	1 hour 20 minutes
C	1.20 pm	2 hours 40 minutes
D	1.45 pm	35 minutes

Studio	Starting time	Session lasts
E	2.25 pm	50 minutes
F	3.50 pm	1 hour 15 minutes
G	4.40 pm	2 hours 35 minutes
H	7.35 pm	2 hours 30 minutes

2 Some programmes are recorded in front of a studio audience.
For each programme find the time when the studio doors open.

	Pop show	Searchers	Laugh-in	Your story	Westenders
Recording starts at	10.55 am	12.05 pm	2.15 pm	3.10 pm	5.05 pm
Doors open	45 minutes before	1 hour 5 minutes before	20 minutes before	1 hour 25 minutes before	1 hour 10 minutes before

3 Find the missing time for each studio.

6TV	RECORDING SCHEDULE			6TV
Studio	**Programme**	**Starts at**	**Records for**	**Finishes at**
A	*The Wheely Bins*	10.15 am	35 minutes	
B	*London Nights*	11.25 am	40 minutes	
C	*Sporting Chance*	12.10 pm	1 hour 55 minutes	
D	*Burnside*		55 minutes	12 noon
E	*The Golden Boys*		50 minutes	1.15 pm
F	*Pinewood Gardens*		1 hour 20 minutes	2.10 pm
G	*Saturday Late*	1.35 pm		4.05 pm
H	*For Ever and Ever*	11.40 am		2.05 pm

Ferry to France

1 Change each time to a 24-hour time.
   (a) 6.20 am   **(b)** 5.15 pm   **(c)** 1.05 pm   **(d)** 2 am   **(e)** 7.55 pm

2 Write each time as a 12-hour time. Use am or pm.
   (a) 11.45   **(b)** 01.10   **(c)** 23.55   **(d)** 20.05   **(e)** 00.15

Class 6 made this Time Diary for the journey to the ferry.

Time Diary: Wednesday	
arrive at school	8.50 am
meet in hall	9.15 am
leave school	10.20 am
picnic lunch	1.40 pm
leave picnic site	2.05 pm
fuel stop	2.45 pm
cross bridge	3.15 pm
arrive at Euro-ferry	4.30 pm

3 What happened at
   (a) 09.15   **(b)** 13.40   **(c)** 14.45   **(d)** 16.30?

4 What happened **just before**
   (a) 10.25   **(b)** 14.50   **(c)** 15.20   **(d)** 09.20?

5 What happened **just after**
   (a) 14.00   **(b)** 10.15   **(c)** 13.35   **(d)** 16.25?

At the port, Class 6 read the ferry sailing times.

FERRIES TO FRANCE	
Sunday	0830
Monday	1205
Tuesday	1350
Wednesday	1830
Thursday	2200
Friday	1115
Saturday	0545

6 On which day does the ferry leave at
   (a) 6.30 pm   **(b)** 11.15 am   **(c)** 1.50 pm?

7 On which days is there a ferry
   (a) before noon   **(b)** after 1.00 pm?

8 The ferry journey takes 6 hours.
   What is the day and time of arrival for
   (a) the Sunday ferry   **(b)** the Thursday ferry?

9

City Tour	
Market	11.15
Tower	13.15
Cathedral	15.15
Theme Park	17.15

Class 6 takes a City Tour.

Where are the children
   (a) at quarter past 3 in the afternoon
   (b) just before 5.20 pm
   (c) just after 1.10 pm?

Drawing shapes

1 For each set of co-ordinates
- mark the points
- join them, in order, to make a shape
- name the shape.

(a) (0, 4) (3, 4) (3, 6) (0, 6)
(b) (5, 3) (6, 5) (9, 6) (8, 4)
(c) (10, 5) (12, 6) (14, 5) (12, 2)
(d) (1, 0) (2, 2) (4, 3) (3, 1)
(e) (6, 2) (10, 3) (10, 1)
(f) (13, 2) (15, 4) (17, 2) (15, 0)

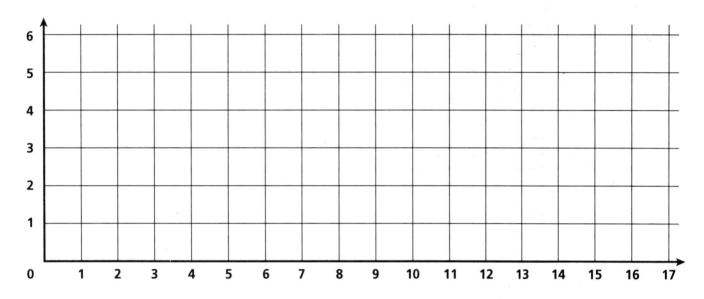

2 Which four-sided shapes have all their sides equal?

_____

3 **(a)** Name each shape and write its co-ordinates.

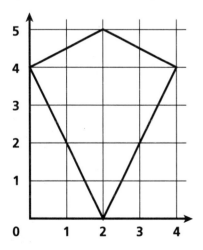

Name _____   _____

Co-ordinates _____   _____

(b) Draw any lines of symmetry on each shape.

Angles

1 Label each of the angles below **acute**, **right** or **obtuse**.

2 **(a)** Cut out each angle.
   (b) Measure each angle using the diagram on **Textbook page 110**.
   (c) Complete this table.

Angle S	acute	40°
Angle T		
Angle U		
Angle V		

Angle W		
Angle X		
Angle Y		
Angle Z		

3 **(a)** Fit **four** pieces together to make a kite.
   (b) Stick the kite in your jotter.

4 **(a)** Fit the other four pieces together to make a four-sided shape.
   (b) Stick the shape in your jotter.

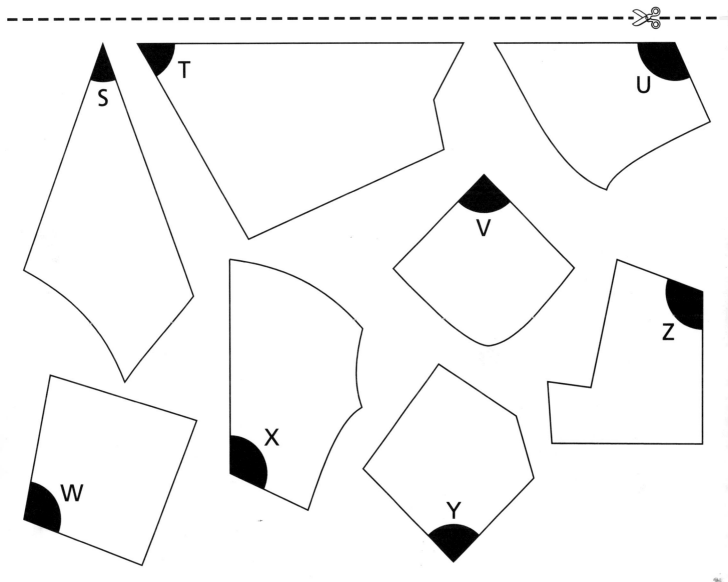

Answers

1 On the beach

1 (a) 53, 141
(b) 37, 127

2 (a) 79 (b) 26 (c) 99 (d) 23 (e) 88
(f) 12 (g) 89 (h) 20 (i) 98 (j) 11

3 (a) 78
(b) 18

4 (a) 65 (b) 35 (c) 92 (d) 8 (e) 96
(f) 17 (g) 84 (h) 24 (i) 87 (j) 33

5 (a) 73
(b) 81
(c) 17
(d) 27

6 (a) 93 (b) 19 (c) 81 (d) 16 (e) 81
(f) 29 (g) 77 (h) 20 (i) 73 (j) 29
(k) 62 (l) 24 (m) 54 (n) 15 (o) 90

2 Large numbers

1 (a) 82 345
(b) 350 000
(c) 400 040
(d) 1 200 000
(e) 3 000 010

2 (a) seventy-three thousand
(b) three hundred and ninety-three thousand, five hundred
(c) two hundred and two thousand, two hundred and two
(d) six million, six hundred

3 (a) 9998, 9999, 10 000
(b) 9000, 10 000, 11 000
(c) 99 900, 100 000, 100 100
(d) 100 090, 100 100, 100 110
(e) 999 999, 1 000 000, 1 000 001

4 (a) 239 156
(b) 249 146
(c) 439 146

5 (a) 761 994
(b) 763 094
(c) 713 994

2 Large numbers – *continued*

6 (a) 25 000 (b) 299 999
(c) 110 010 (d) 77 690
(e) 91 000 (f) 1 000 400
(g) 140 473 (h) 49 001

7 (a) 20 000 (b) 2000 (c) 2 000 000
(d) 70 000 (e) 400 000 (f) 600
(g) 400 000 (h) 10 000 (i) 5000

3 On the reef

1 (a) 11 632 (b) 10 001 (c) 10 201

2 (a) 6000 (b) 10 661 (c) 7070 (d) 11 203
(e) 15 626

3 (a) 8024 (b) 7850 (c) 1933

4 (a) 1848 (b) 2048 (c) 1431

5 (a) 2763 (b) 3125 (c) 1944 (d) 1752
(e) 682 (f) 2246 (g) 2162 (h) 1410
(i) 6577 (j) 2694

6 (a) 8257, 10 930
(b) 2673
(c) 1070

4 Diving for treasure

1 Air: about 300 litres   Fuel: about 900 litres
Depth: about 100 metres
Diving time: about 500 minutes

2 (a) 500 (b) 400 (c) 100 (d) 1000
(e) 900 (f) 300

3 (a) 600 (b) 700 (c) 500 (d) 700
(e) 600 (f) 500 (g) 300 (h) 500
(i) 400 (j) 500

4 (a) 190 (b) 120 (c) 30 (d) 70

5 (a) 190 (b) 270 (c) 240 (d) 330
(e) 320 (f) 260 (g) 330 (h) 90
(i) 220 (j) 160 or 170

6 (a) 90
(b) 260

1   **(a)** £9591   **(b)** £8598   **(c)** £9576   **(d)** £7470

2   8660 zips, 7670 buttons, 9672 rolls of cloth, 13 678 reels of thread

3   **(a)** 19 000   **(b)** 9395   **(c)** 19 377   **(d)** 19 348

4   **(a)** 8982 metres of cloth
     (b) 11 976 buttons

5   **(a)** 17 276   **(b)** 12 340   **(c)** 19 744

6   8052

7

	(a) 6 trips	(b) 9 trips	(c) 7 trips
coats	9768	14 652	11 396
hats	5388	8082	6286
anoraks	18 642	27 963	21 749

1   **(a)** 152 r 2   **(b)** 147 r 2   **(c)** 428 r 1
     (d) 197 r 4

2   **(a)** 678 r 1   **(b)** 878 r 1   **(c)** 842 r 1
     (d) 810 r 1   **(e)** 899 r 2   **(f)** 1493
     (g) 415 r 4   **(h)** 3767 r 1

3   **(a)** 1520 r 1   **(b)** 912 r 1   **(c)** 1140 r 1

4   **(a)** 3649   **(b)** 2689   **(c)** 1736
     (d) 1834   **(e)** 1502 r 1   **(f)** 607
     (g) 1744 r 2   **(h)** 4938

5

	(a)	(b)	(c)	(d)
	2 trucks	3 trucks	4 trucks	5 trucks
lamps	3477	2318	1738 and 2 left over	1390 and 4 left over
blankets	1503 and 1 left over	1002 and 1 left over	751 and 3 left over	601 and 2 left over
tents	2134 and 1 left over	1423	1067	853 and 4 left over

6   369

7   3015

1   **(a)** £165   **(b)** £139   **(c)** £107   **(d)** £79

2   **(a)** 298 r 1   **(b)** 156 r 6   **(c)** 318 r 1
     (d) 504 r 3   **(e)** 1046 r 4   **(f)** 1066 r 6
     (g) 1228 r 6   **(h)** 1084 r 1

3   **(a)** 1248 and 1 left over
     (b) 970 and 7 left over

4   **(a)** 1147   **(b)** 756   **(c)** 843
     (d) 1027   **(e)** 653 r 4   **(f)** 821 r 1
     (g) 493 r 5   **(h)** 974 r 2

5   **(a)** 345 and 5 left over
     (b) 259 and 3 left over

6   786 and 4 pens left over
     429 and 1 ring left over
     127 and 3 clocks left over
     138 and 2 watches left over

7   **(a)** Yes. It divides exactly with no remainder.
     (b) No. There is a remainder of 4.

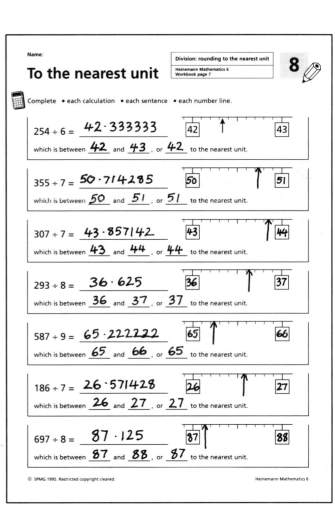

Name:

Division: rounding to the nearest unit

To the nearest unit   Heinemann Mathematics 6   Workbook page 7   **8**

Complete • each calculation • each sentence • each number line.

$254 \div 6 =$ _42·333333_   [42] ↑ [43]
which is between _42_ and _43_, or _42_ to the nearest unit.

$355 \div 7 =$ _50·714285_   [50] ↑ [51]
which is between _50_ and _51_, or _51_ to the nearest unit.

$307 \div 7 =$ _43·857142_   [43] ↑ [44]
which is between _43_ and _44_, or _44_ to the nearest unit.

$293 \div 8 =$ _36·625_   [36] ↑ [37]
which is between _36_ and _37_, or _37_ to the nearest unit.

$587 \div 9 =$ _65·222222_   [65] ↑ [66]
which is between _65_ and _66_, or _65_ to the nearest unit.

$186 \div 7 =$ _26·571428_   [26] ↑ [27]
which is between _26_ and _27_, or _27_ to the nearest unit.

$697 \div 8 =$ _87·125_   [87] ↑ [88]
which is between _87_ and _88_, or _87_ to the nearest unit.

    Heinemann Mathematics 6

9 Catching the flight

1 (a) 17   (b) 13   (c) 12   (d) 9

2 (a) 43   (b) 56   (c) 259   (d) 260

3 (a) 32   (b) 29   (c) 26   (d) 35

4 (a) 6   (b) 9   (c) 57   (d) 29

5 (a) Glasgow – 16 kg
   Singapore – 16 kg
   Toronto – 20 kg
   (b) Glasgow – 39 cases
   Singapore – 42 cases
   Toronto – 29 cases

10 Equal fractions

1 (a) $\frac{1}{2} = \frac{2}{4}$ (b) $\frac{2}{5} = \frac{4}{10}$ (c) $\frac{1}{2} = \frac{3}{6}$
   (d) $\frac{1}{4} = \frac{2}{8}$ (e) $\frac{3}{4} = \frac{15}{20}$ (f) $\frac{3}{10} = \frac{6}{20}$
   (g) $\frac{5}{6} = \frac{10}{12}$ (h) $\frac{2}{3} = \frac{6}{9}$

2 (a) 3   (b) 5   (c) 4

3 (a) $\frac{1}{2} = \frac{4}{8}$ (b) $\frac{2}{3} = \frac{4}{6}$ (c) $\frac{1}{2} = \frac{6}{12}$
   (d) $\frac{1}{10} = \frac{10}{100}$ (e) $\frac{1}{5} = \frac{3}{12}$ (f) $\frac{3}{5} = \frac{6}{10}$
   (g) $\frac{4}{5} = \frac{16}{20}$ (h) $\frac{1}{4} = \frac{5}{20}$ (i) $\frac{7}{10} = \frac{14}{20}$
   (j) $\frac{4}{5} = \frac{8}{10}$ (k) $\frac{3}{4} = \frac{9}{12}$ (l) $\frac{9}{10} = \frac{90}{100}$

4 (a) $\frac{6}{8}$ (b) $\frac{8}{12}$ (c) $\frac{30}{100}$

11 Equal fractions

1 (a) $\frac{2}{6} = \frac{1}{3}$ (b) $\frac{4}{8} = \frac{1}{2}$
   (c) $\frac{9}{12} = \frac{3}{4}$ (d) $\frac{8}{10} = \frac{4}{5}$

2 (a) $\frac{5}{10} = \frac{1}{2}$ (b) $\frac{3}{9} = \frac{1}{3}$ (c) $\frac{3}{12} = \frac{1}{4}$
   (d) $\frac{10}{20} = \frac{1}{2}$ (e) $\frac{6}{9} = \frac{2}{3}$ (f) $\frac{8}{12} = \frac{2}{3}$
   (g) $\frac{30}{100} = \frac{3}{10}$ (h) $\frac{18}{20} = \frac{9}{10}$

3 (a) $\frac{1}{2}$ (b) $\frac{3}{4}$ (c) $\frac{1}{3}$
   (d) $\frac{2}{5}$ (e) $\frac{3}{4}$ (f) $\frac{2}{5}$

4 (a) $\frac{2}{3}$ (b) $\frac{1}{4}$ (c) $\frac{3}{5}$ (d) $\frac{1}{5}$ (e) $\frac{1}{4}$
   (f) $\frac{5}{6}$ (g) $\frac{4}{5}$ (h) $\frac{1}{2}$ (i) $\frac{3}{5}$ (j) $\frac{7}{10}$

5 (a) $\frac{1}{2}$ (b) $\frac{1}{6}$

6 Sunday $\frac{1}{10}$ Monday $\frac{1}{5}$ Tuesday $\frac{1}{4}$

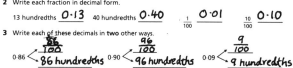

Name:

Division: second decimal place, notation
Heinemann Mathematics 6
Workbook page 10

12 ✏

Allt Bridge signs

1 Each sign has 100 light cells.
How much of each sign is lit? Write your answer
• as a fraction • in decimal form.

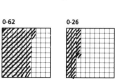 $\frac{51}{100}$ 0·51 $\frac{30}{100}$ 0·30

2 Write each fraction in decimal form.
13 hundredths __0·13__   40 hundredths __0·40__ $\frac{1}{100}$ __0·01__ $\frac{10}{100}$ __0·10__

3 Write each of these decimals in **two** other ways.
0·86 — $\frac{86}{100}$, 86 hundredths   0·90 — $\frac{96}{100}$, 96 hundredths   0·09 — $\frac{9}{100}$, 9 hundredths

4 Each sign has 100 light cells.
Colour to show the given fraction.
0·62   0·26   0·06   0·50   0·99

5 Colour to show the given amount.
1·42   2·20

6 Write in decimal form:
3 units and 22 hundredths __3·22__   4 units and 70 hundredths __4·70__
3 units and 3 hundredths __3·03__   5 units and 49 hundredths __5·49__

    Heinemann Mathematics 6

---

13 Plants and posts

1 (a) 0·48 = 4 tenths and 8 hundredths
   (b) 0·26 = 2 tenths and 6 hundredths
   (c) 0·77 = 7 tenths and 7 hundredths
   (d) 0·60 = 6 tenths and 0 hundredths
   (e) 0·07 = 0 tenths and 7 hundredths

2 (a) 0·36   (b) 0·58   (c) 0·20   (d) 0·09
   (e) 0·11

3 (a) 0·67 = 0·6 + 0·07
   (b) 0·37 = 0·3 + 0·07
   (c) 0·80 = 0·8 + 0·00
   (d) 0·04 = 0·0 + 0·04
   (e) 0·66 = 0·6 + 0·06

4 (a) 0·22 m, 0·29 m   (b) 22 cm, 29 cm

5 (a) 3 hundredths   (b) 3 tens   (c) 3 tenths
   (d) 3 units

6 (a) 3·06, 0·63, 0·36, 3·60, 6·03
   (b) 6·03, 3·60, 3·06, 0·63, 0·36
   (c) 3·06 and 0·63

7 (a) 0·5, 0·55, 5·05, 5·5, 5·55
   (b) 0·60, 0·81, 1·08, 1·68, 1·8

8 (a) Q   (b) S

1 (a) 0·54 (b) 0·67 (c) 0·43 (d) 0·72

2 (a) 0·94 (b) 3·1 (c) 10·97 (d) 54·71
(e) 33·44 (f) 64·74

3 (a) 22·11 m (b) 17·86 m (c) 16·04 m

4 (a) 2·88 (b) 3·49 (c) 4·37 (d) 8·88
(e) 11·89 (f) 27·27 (g) 13·37 (h) 41·86
(i) 0·67 (j) 37·09

5 (a) £9·05 (b) £6·54 (c) £10·19 (d) £29·66

6 (a) £14·60 (b) £40·38 (c) £30·19

7 £70·66

1 (a) $\frac{1}{2}$ 50% (b) $\frac{1}{4}$ 25%
(c) $\frac{1}{10}$ 10%

2 (a) 50% = $\frac{1}{2}$ (b) 25% = $\frac{1}{4}$ (c) 10% = $\frac{1}{10}$

3 (a) 7 (b) 11 (c) 20 (d) 3
(e) 7 (f) 12 (g) 5 (h) 9
(i) 3 (j) 17 (k) 14 (l) 10

4 (a) 170 castle pencils, 54 bendy pencils
(b) 85 castle pencils, 27 bendy pencils

5 (a) 150 (b) 30

6 (a) 40 medium quilts, 8 large quilts
(b) 40%

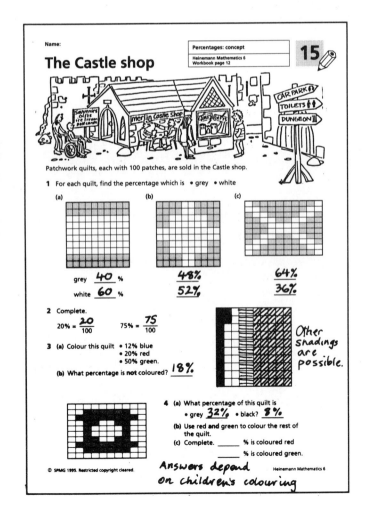

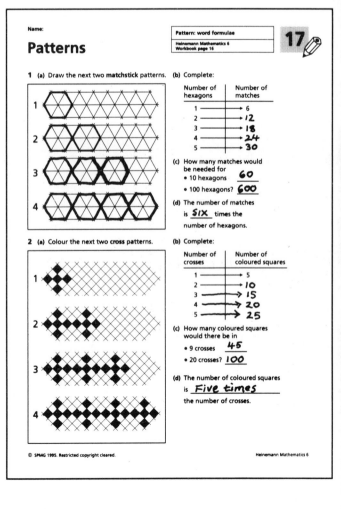

18 Departure lounges

1
```
    23
  × 16
  ────
   138
 + 230
  ────
   368
```

2 (a) 276 (b) 322 (c) 391

3 (a) 608 (b) 611 (c) 915 (d) 928
(e) 814 (f) 828 (g) 522 (h) 561

4 (a) 735 (b) 882

5 (a) white 385, pink 231, peach 506
(b) white 455, pink 273, peach 598

19 Playing the game

1
```
    45
  × 27
  ────
   315
 + 900
  ────
  1215
```

2 (a) 1035 (b) 1961 (c) 2236 (d) 3976
(e) 2418

3 (a) 990 (b) 2052 (c) 2204 (d) 1476
(e) 1260

4 (a) £1118 (b) £3515 (c) £5544 (d) £2448

5 (a) £1176 (b) £1672 (c) £1537

6 (a) 1116 (b) 1075 (c) 532
(d) 972 (e) 2479 (f) 1488

20 Going on board

1
```
18 ⌐60
  −18 │1
  ────
    42│
  −18 │1
  ────
    24│
  −18 │1
  ────
     6│3
```
There are **3** magazines for each plane and **6** left over.

2 (a) 2 r 6 (b) 3 r 7 (c) 2 r 9

20 Going on board – *continued*

3
```
14 ⌐163
 −140 │10
 ─────
    23│
  −14 │1
 ─────
     9│11
```
There are **11** copies for each plane and **9** left over.

4 (a) 11 r 13 (b) 10 r 13 (c) 11 r 19
(d) 12 r 10 (e) 11 r 3 (f) 11

5 There are **22** packs for each plane and **4** left over.

6 (a) 21 r 12 (b) 21 r 8 (c) 20 r 20
(d) 12 (e) 31 r 21 (f) 21 r 8

21 Spick and span

1 13 teams

2 (a) 12 (b) 20 (c) 31

3 (a) 20 dispensers
(b) 20 bars are left over.

4 12

5 21

6 £22

22 Lengths

1 (a) 465 cm (b) 1020 cm (c) 506 cm
(d) 308 cm

2 (a) 345 cm (b) 390 cm (c) 705 cm
(d) 450 cm

3 (a) 2 m 65 cm (b) 3 m 81 cm
(c) 3 m 40 cm (d) 5 m 50 cm
(e) 8 m 7 cm (f) 6 m 5 cm
(g) 2 m 30 cm (h) 3 m 6 cm

4 (a) 30 m (b) 32 m (c) $27\frac{1}{2}$ m
(d) 28 m (e) 22 m 15 cm (f) 23 m 43 cm

5 (a) 12 m (b) 18 m (c) 23 m

6 (a) 28 m (b) 2 m 48 cm (c) 12 m 40 cm
(d) 17 m (e) 24 m 36 cm (f) 10 m

Just weight

1 Read the scales to find the weight of each of these.

Ⓑ berries **400g**　　Ⓢ swede **1kg 600g**　　Ⓡ raisins **125g**

Ⓐ apple **375g**　　Ⓝ nuts **75g**　　Ⓖ grapes **190g**

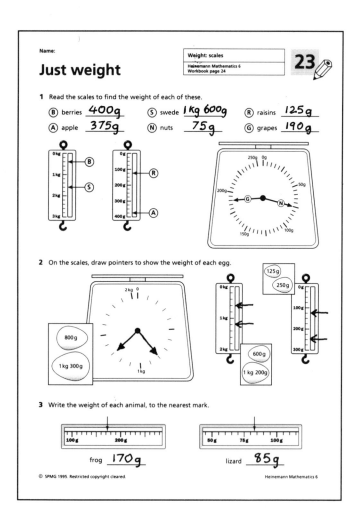

2 On the scales, draw pointers to show the weight of each egg.

3 Write the weight of each animal, to the nearest mark.

frog **170g**　　　　lizard **85g**

　　　　Heinemann Mathematics 6

Medicines

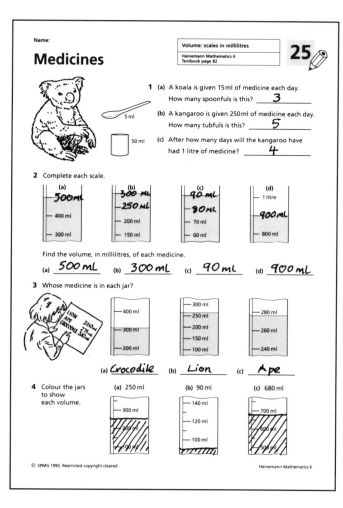

1 (a) A koala is given 15 ml of medicine each day.
How many spoonfuls is this? **3**

(b) A kangaroo is given 250 ml of medicine each day.
How many tubfuls is this? **5**

(c) After how many days will the kangaroo have
had 1 litre of medicine? **4**

2 Complete each scale.

Find the volume, in millilitres, of each medicine.

(a) **500 mL**　(b) **300 mL**　(c) **90 mL**　(d) **900 mL**

3 Whose medicine is in each jar?

(a) **Crocodile**　(b) **Lion**　(c) **Ape**

4 Colour the jars to show each volume.
(a) 250 ml　(b) 90 ml　(c) 680 ml

　　　　Heinemann Mathematics 6

More designs

Divide each design into squares and rectangles and find its area.

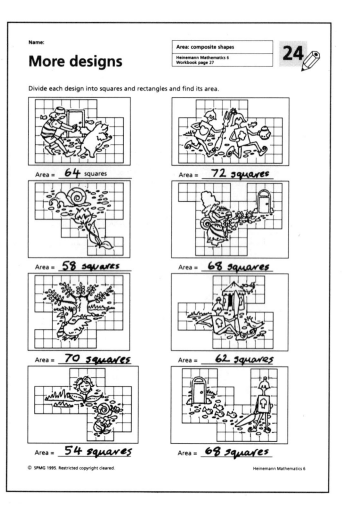

Area = **64** squares　　　Area = **72 squares**

Area = **58 squares**　　　Area = **68 squares**

Area = **70 squares**　　　Area = **62 squares**

Area = **54 squares**　　　Area = **68 squares**

　　　　Heinemann Mathematics 6

26　Radio station

1 (a) 40 minutes　(b) 45 minutes
(c) 50 minutes

2 (a) 1 hour 35 minutes　(b) 1 hour 45 minutes
(c) 1 hour 50 minutes　(d) 1 hour 50 minutes

3 (a) 11.35 am　(b) 12.15 pm　(c) 12.40 pm

4 (a) Sports day　1 hour 40 minutes
(b) Baby show　1 hour 50 minutes
(c) Lifeboats　3 hours 50 minutes
(d) Royal visit　3 hours 30 minutes
(e) Speedway　5 hours 50 minutes

5 9 hours 50 minutes

6 10 hours 20 minutes

1
A	9.55 am	E	3.15 pm
B	11.35 am	F	5.05 pm
C	4.00 pm	G	7.15 pm
D	2.20 pm	H	10.05 pm

2 Pop Show 10.10 am   Searchers 11.00 am
Laugh-in 1.55 pm   Your Story 1.45 pm
Westenders 3.55 pm

3
A	10.50 am
B	12.05 pm
C	2.05 pm
D	11.05 am
E	12.25 pm
F	12.50 pm
G	2 hours 30 minutes
H	2 hours 25 minutes

28 Ferry to France

1 **(a)** 06.20   **(b)** 17.15   **(c)** 13.05
(d) 02.00   **(e)** 19.55

2 **(a)** 11.45 am   **(b)** 1.10 am   **(c)** 11.55 pm
(d) 8.05 pm   **(e)** 12.15 am

3 **(a)** met in hall   **(b)** picnic lunch
(c) fuel stop   **(d)** arrived at Euro-ferry

4 **(a)** left school   **(b)** fuel stop
(c) crossed bridge   **(d)** met in hall

5 **(a)** left picnic site   **(b)** left school
(c) picnic lunch   **(d)** arrived at Euro-ferry

6 **(a)** Wednesday **(b)** Friday **(c)** Tuesday

7 **(a)** Sunday, Friday, Saturday
(b) Tuesday, Wednesday, Thursday

8 **(a)** Sunday at 14.30 **(b)** Friday at 04.00

9 **(a)** Cathedral
(b) Theme Park
(c) Tower

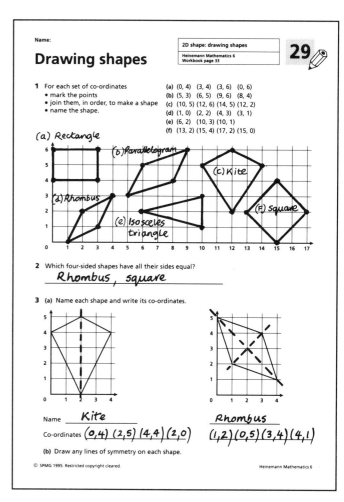

Name:

2D shape: drawing shapes
Heinemann Mathematics 6
Workbook page 33

29

Drawing shapes

1 For each set of co-ordinates
• mark the points
• join them, in order, to make a shape
• name the shape.

(a) (0, 4) (3, 4) (3, 6) (0, 6)
(b) (5, 3) (6, 5) (9, 6) (8, 4)
(c) (10, 5) (12, 6) (14, 5) (12, 2)
(d) (1, 0) (2, 2) (4, 3) (3, 1)
(e) (6, 2) (10, 3) (10, 1)
(f) (13, 2) (15, 4) (17, 2) (15, 0)

(a) Rectangle   (b) Parallelogram   (c) Kite
(d) Rhombus   (e) Isosceles triangle   (f) Square

2 Which four-sided shapes have all their sides equal?
Rhombus, square

3 (a) Name each shape and write its co-ordinates.

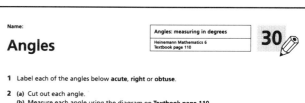

Name Kite
Co-ordinates (0,4) (2,5) (4,4) (2,0)

Rhombus
(1,2) (0,5) (3,4) (4,1)

(b) Draw any lines of symmetry on each shape.

© SPMG 1995. Restricted copyright cleared.   Heinemann Mathematics 6

Name:

Angles: measuring in degrees
Heinemann Mathematics 6
Textbook page 110

30

Angles

1 Label each of the angles below **acute**, **right** or **obtuse**.

2 (a) Cut out each angle.
(b) Measure each angle using the diagram on **Textbook page 110**.
(c) Complete this table.

Angle S	acute	40°
Angle T	acute	60°
Angle U	obtuse	115°
Angle V	right	90°

Angle W	obtuse	100°
Angle X	obtuse	115°
Angle Y	right	90°
Angle Z	obtuse	110°

3 (a) Fit **four** pieces together to make a kite.
(b) Stick the kite in your jotter.

4 (a) Fit the other four pieces together to make a four-sided shape.
(b) Stick the shape in your jotter.

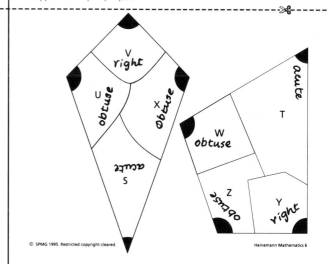

© SPMG 1995. Restricted copyright cleared.   Heinemann Mathematics 6